Light & Stone

Highlights from the Scott Gem Collection

Photography by
Harold and Erica Van Pelt

Commentary by
Peter C. Keller, Ph. D.
and
Michael M. Scott

Close-up of Tanzanite Crystal

© 2002 The Bowers Museum of Cultural Art
The Bowers Museum of Cultural Art
2002 North Main St.
Santa Ana, California, 92706
Telephone: 714 567 3600
www.bowers.org

ISBN: 0-9679612-2-X

Sculptors
Gerd Dreher
John Marshall, Silversmith
Bernd Munsteiner, Fantasy Cuts
Gunter Petry
H. Postler
Dieter Roth

Photography by: Harold and Erica Van Pelt
Design by: ThinkDesign, Buellton, CA
Color Scans by: Digital Impressions, Milpitas, CA
Printed by: George Rice & Sons, A Quebecor
World Company, Los Angeles, CA

Cover:
"Repose"
Gunter Petry - 1991
Idar-Oberstein, Germany

Back cover:
Tanzanite Crystal Close-up
Tanzania

Inside Front and Back covers:
Black Opal Close-up
Lightning Ridge, Australia

Close-up of Burmese Ruby Crystal

TABLE OF CONTENTS

FOREWORD

From a curatorial perspective, the opportunity to work with, and ultimately present an exhibition of a "world class" collection to the public could be considered the epitome of one's professional career. It really doesn't matter if it's a collection of butterflies, paintings or anything else that is considered collectable; it's an incredible experience. However, imagine the excitement when the collection being presented is gemstones! Gems have been called earth's most perfect distillates. They are the rarest, most beautiful, yet durable minerals that are known to man. They have been worn as items of adornment for almost a hundred centuries. It has been said that nowhere else can a greater concentration of wealth be seen in a smaller amount of space. Gems have been kept during times of turmoil because a million dollars can easily fit into a small pocket. Try that with gold!

The Scott Collection is arguably the most important private gem collection in the United States, and has few rivals in the world outside of the royal families. Our exhibition of Light & Stone is one of the most important exhibitions of gems ever presented by an American museum. The Bowers Museum is very proud to have the opportunity to organize this very ambitious exhibition, and to share it with the American people. Light & Stone illustrates the rarely presented diversity found in many gem species. Virtually the entire known color range from diamonds, sapphires, tourmalines, garnets, and beryls are shown. What's more, they are shown in qualities and sizes scarcely seen. I was particularly impressed by the collection of very rare Paraiba tourmalines; the 242 ct. tanzanite, thought to be the world's largest; the 400 ct. golden sapphire; the superb 10 ct. Burmese ruby; the 64.55 ct. intense blue sapphire; 16 ct. "Padparadscha" the rarest of all colors; two of the world's largest tsavorite garnets at 45 ct. and 32 ct. In addition, for those who appreciate history and large diamonds, the exhibition includes a 21.25 ct. diamond from the historic Golconda mines in India. It's important to note that the exhibition includes a significant selection of gem crystals; gems "in the rough", just as they came out of the ground. Many who know these crystals feel they are as beautiful as their faceted counterparts.

The second half of the exhibition is dedicated to gems as works of art. This includes contemporary sculptures from Germany. One of the definite highlights of the Scott Collection is the work of master carver Bernd Munsteiner of Idar-Oberstein, Germany. Munsteiner's work has redefined how gemstones can be faceted to best interact with light as sculptures that range in size from a few carats to over 200 pounds! Finally, the Scott Collection includes sculptures by a Seattle-based contemporary artist and metalsmith John Marshall. These pieces combine natural gem crystals, sculptural pieces themselves, with magnificent silver pieces worked in very unique ways.

This exhibition is a rare opportunity for the public to see a very private collection. I have no doubt that it will be an inspiration to all who see it and will stimulate an appreciation of both the natural world and beauty that has been created by the hand of man.

Peter C. Keller, Ph. D.
President
The Bowers Museum of Cultural Art

Opposite:
Close-up of Nigerian Emerald Crystals

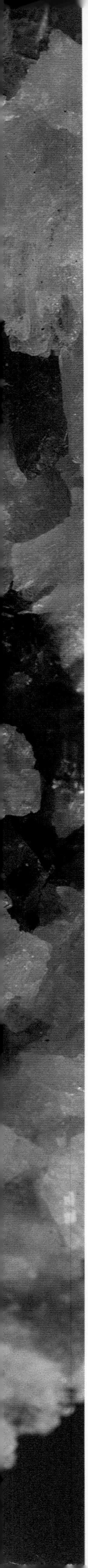

DEDICATION

Harold and Erica Van Pelt

For their decade of success in capturing the story of the collection on film, an extremely difficult challenge. Some say that their work is so good that it makes an object look better than it is. Hopefully viewers of this exhibition will agree that, "What you see *is* what you get!"

Dr. Eduard J. Gubelin

The grandfather of modern gemology, for surveying the collection, selecting the more important pieces and writing personal letters of attestation in his enviable and inspirational style.

Dr. Peter C. Keller

For his vision and decisiveness by taking the risk of publicly showing the collection as art, not as part of an earth science exhibit. Thank you for your courage in the face of bureaucracy in creating this milestone in the appreciation of gemstones.

Michael M. Scott
Los Altos, California

Opposite:
Close-up of California Spessartite Garnet Crystal

THE PHOTOGRAPHERS

Most people today have personal experience with candid photography of ordinary opaque objects--objects that light cannot penetrate. Windowpanes are designed to be invisible. Imagine the difficulty of photographing the windowpane itself! A gemstone is a "light computer". Its shape provides two major functions: the front side acts like small lens, collecting incoming light from different directions while the back acts like small mirrors with light from the front reflected from one back side to the other and then reflected back out of the front of the gemstone. The light is "purified" and altered during this passage through the stone. Few have ever mastered how to photograph jewels.

For over 30 years, the husband and wife team of Harold and Erica Van Pelt has been synonymous with the world's finest gem and mineral photography. Their spectacular photographs have graced the covers of every major gem and mineral journal in the world and have added color and excitement to over a dozen books.

The Van Pelts are dedicated professionals, sometimes spending untold hours perfecting a single shot, occasionally under very unusual circumstances. Perhaps one of the most unusual examples was in Colombia, South America, while on assignment for Smithsonian Magazine. They endured an entire week in the claustrophobic confines of a vault in the core of the historic Popayan Cathedral where they were asked to document its famous bejeweled religious treasures. However, even in their Hollywood studio, the Van Pelts go to great lengths to seek perfection. To accomplish the perfection for which they are so well known, they spend hours setting up a shot. Each gem is checked to make certain that there are no fingerprints or dust, perfectly oriented and ideally lit. Then, they take a black and white Polaroid check shot to determine the best exposure setting. When they are both satisfied, they take the final shot using large format 4 x 5 color transparency, never 35mm.

Their favorite shots are those showing "rough and cut", the natural gem crystal along side its faceted counterpart. They appreciate the rarity and beauty of such pairings, as well as educational value. Their trademark is to capture the precise color of each stone in a large and diverse suite of colored gems, all together at the same time and under the same light. Each gem must show brilliant details and perfect focus.

For the past 10 years, the Van Pelts have enthusiastically pursued the exciting challenge associated with the privilege of documenting one of the finest "rough and cut" gem and gem sculpture collections developed in the 20th century: the Scott collection. This book is a testament to their passion and skill--the ultimate in photographic perfection.

Opposite:
This Dragonfly Pin with Diamonds and Rubies contains 17 Demantoid Garnets.

"Merelani Magic"
This bolo tie was created especially for Mr. Scott and featurea a large Tanzanite Cabochon that weights 126.83 ct. (Cabochon means a stone has a curved polished surface rather than flat facets.) Made in 18 kt. Gold that is engraved and enameled orange, it is accented with orange Namibian Spessartite Garnets total weight of 3.10 ct. and Diamonds with a total weight of 3.70 ct.
Silverhorn, Santa Barbara, California

COLLECTION NOTES

"You may NOT wear any jewelry, especially rings."

My ninth grade teacher said this in the first class I had using a computer. It was a state-of-the-art vacuum tube IBM 650 model controlled by feeding it thin, uniformly stacked, punched cardboard cards. No chad allowed! The teacher worried that a ring on a finger might make a ding onto a side of the card stack, causing a jam in the ultra high-speed reader and an enormous mess. Many years later, after retiring as the first president of Apple Computer, I was finished with computers and could finally have a nice ring. It should be green; emerald would be too common. Tsavorite garnet was selected and a local custom jeweler had a selection shipped in. A certification from an independent laboratory was ordered on this expensive 5 ct. jewel. It came back that it was a "YAG", a man-made synthetic laser mineral worth only a tiny fraction of the stone I was intending to buy. Thus, my new interest formed requiring new studies in science, travel, beauty and business. I would become a collector.

Anyone can be a collector. Specimens vary widely in size, price, color, type, structure, location, etc. In fact, the most perfect that nature makes are the smallest and cheapest! Creating "large, clean and flawless" stones are much more difficult for nature. Start "small" (literally) with affordable thumbnail sized specimens that can be displayed in inexpensive cubic one-inch plastic boxes with magnifying lenses molded permanently into their tops. A new collector should choose a single specific species to start with and try collecting its full range of colors. For an extra challenge, one might try starting by collecting only a single pleasing shape. Anyone can begin a collection they will be proud of this way and not have to spent a lot of money.

Naturally, money and jewels have a long and close relation to each other. However, the pricing and selling of the stones can be an interesting science onto itself. Economists speak of supply and demand as being the balance of markets. In the collector's gemstone market, there is no supply (or, I should say, a very minute supply) and almost no demand because almost no one knows about them and because they are so scarce. When buying where only two or three pieces may be in existence in the world, the rules are very flexible and the seller may have valuable knowledge that the buyer does not. When you are a buyer of stones, you have something that is even more precious than the stone itself is to the seller -money. Remember that a 2 ct. stone appears to be only forty percent larger than a 1 ct. stone but can cost much more than twice as much and a 9 ct. stone might cost only sixty percent of a 10 ct. one. Finally, one must be willing NOT to buy "the finest ever" or the "only one of its kind."

My goal has been to collect quality and beauty…and for the collection to tell the emotional story of the impact of colors.

Michael M. Scott
Los Altos, California

Rubies and Sapphires

Emerald and Other Beryls

Tourmalines

Demantoids, Tsavorites, and Other Rare Garnets

Tanzanite

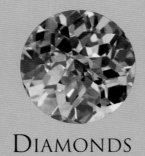

Diamonds

PART I
GEM AND
CRYSTAL TREASURES

When the ancients first discovered the beauty and importance of gem materials, they utilized the gem crystal's unaltered state from the way they were found. It wasn't until sometime around the 14th century that mankind could improve on a diamond crystal's beauty by adding more surfaces through a grinding process that is now called faceting. Yet when we look at many of the natural gem crystals, we understand just how wonderful these natural sculptures can be, and now in many respects, they are even rarer than their faceted counterparts.

Color, another factor in the beauty of gemstones, is not as clear-cut as history would lead us to believe. While many gems are thought of as being associated with a unique color, this isn't the case. Sapphire isn't always blue; in fact, it can be virtually any color of the rainbow, as can tourmaline, the beryls, and with the exception of blue, the garnets. So we can appreciate when looking at the Scott Collection, the full color range of most of the important gems, as well as rare colors such as green tanzanites, Paraiba tourmalines, and red diamonds.

Editor's Note:

Carrots, Karats or Carats?
Carrots are the familiar orange root vegetable. The Karat is a unit of proportion of gold in a metal alloy equal to one twenty-fourth part pure gold thus 18-karat gold means that the metal alloy contains seventy-five percent gold. It is abbreviated "kt." The Carat is a unit of weight for gemstones possibly based on the weight of a Carob seed. Today a Carat is defined to be exactly one-fifth of a metric gram or 200 milligrams. A handful of 2270 one-carat diamonds weighs one pound. Carat is abbreviated "ct."

RUBIES AND SAPPHIRES

Ruby and sapphire are varieties of the mineral corundum, which is color-less as pure aluminum oxide. However, very small amounts of elemental impurities such as iron, magnesium, or chromium can act as coloring agents allowing ruby to be red and all other colors of the spectrum to be sapphire. This clarification isn't without controversy since gemologists often have difficulty defining the line between a pink (light red) sapphire and a pale ruby. Blue sapphires are best known, but by no means are they the rarest. That honor belongs to the pinkish-orange variety known as "Padparadscha", the Singhalese word for lotus blossom as allusion to its color. The finest rubies are the so-called pigeon blood stones from Mogok, Burma, although excellent rubies also come from Thailand, Tanzania and Vietnam. The "gem island" of Sri Lanka is best known for it's production of sapphires, but Burma, Tanzania, Thailand and Cambodia are also significant producers. The finest blue sapphires historically come from the Himalayan region of Kashmir.

Opposite:
Ruby Crystal
1730 ct.
Mogok, Burma
1 ct. faceted Ruby shown
for scale

Common Sapphire Crystals
up to 700 ct.
Sri Lanka (Ceylon)
1 ct. faceted stone shown
for scale

Opposite:
Colors of Sapphire and Ruby
1 to 29 ct.
Worldwide Localities

Guarded Treasure
Natural Royal Blue Sapphire
guarded by solid Gold Cobra
64 ct.
Sri Lanka (Ceylon)

Opposite. Right:
"Ceylon Sinflower"
Can a jewel ever be too large or heavy
for one to wear? Very few have ever
worn anything this sinful!..This
awesome 400.06 ct. yellow Ceylon
Sapphire is mounted in 18 kt Red Gold
and accented with Diamonds. When
one tires of the necklace, the centerpiece detaches and mounts on a stem
becoming an Object d'Art Flower in a
Rock Quartz Crystal vase.
Silverhorn, Santa Barbara, California

What is Beauty?
Orchid Flower Sapphire Brooch with Spinels, Diamonds
and Demantoid Garnets in Titanium is an extraordinary
example of modern design with Sapphires of total
weight 33 ct. from Montana and Burma
ESG Jewelers, Basel, Switzerland

Opposite:
"Pigeon Blood Red"
Considered one of the finest rubies in the
world, this Ruby and Diamond Ring displays
the "top" color of Red
10.07 ct.
Mogok, Burma

EMERALD AND OTHER BERYLS

Emerald is the most desirable form or "variety" of the mineral beryl. It is no different than other less expensive beryls except for very small amounts of chromium that gives it its characteristic rich green color. If the beryl is pure, and totally lacking in impurities, it is known as goshenite and colorless. Small amounts of manganese yields a pink variety known as morganite, named after the 19th century industrialist J.P. Morgan. Iron gives us the sea blue-green beryl known as aquamarine.

The state of Minas Gerais, Brazil is historically one of our richest sources for beryls other than emeralds. The finest emeralds have come from the mines at Muzo and Chivor in Colombia since the 16th century. Romans mined emeralds in Egypt. Later sources included Russia, South Africa, and India. Recently a new even rarer "red emerald" was discovered in the Wah Wah Mountains of Utah. This new variety is still a "collector's stone" and has yet to be commercially named, although it has all the physical characteristic of an emerald except for its color.

Opposite:
Perfect!
Aquamarine Crystal with white Cleavelandite
Nature at her best is hand-mined ...no dynamite, no backhoes
3 in. high
Pakistan

Emeralds from the Gachala Mine, Colombia
A cutter must start with a very large and clean piece of rough, like the one shown here, to cut a finished gemstone like this faceted cushion cut one. Usually 70 to 80 percent of the original weight is lost in faceting!
32 ct. faceted Emerald
187 ct. "Rough" but gemmy Emerald crystal
Colombia

Emeralds from Western Africa
100 ct. oval cabochon
2 to 30 ct. faceted gemstones
3 in. long doubly terminated crystal
Nigeria

Opposite:
Colors of Beryl
Pink Morganite, blue Aquamarine, colorless Goshenite, red Beryl, green Beryl, and Emerald are all different varieties of the mineral Beryl.
2 to 48 ct.
Madagascar, Brazil, the United States and Colombia

Emeralds from the Muzo Mine, Colombia
The Muzo Mine, Boyaca, Colombia, has produced the finest Emeralds
in the world since its discovery in 1537. This extraordinary two inch
matrix specimen testifies to the mines undisputed reputation.
Colombia
1 and 30 ct. faceted Emeralds shown for scale

Gemstone Giants
Beryls, Tourmalines and Spodumenes
113 to 333 ct.
Afghanistan, Brazil and Mozambique

"Red Emerald"
This rare and beautiful relative of Emerald is
found exclusively in the Wah Wah Mountains of Utah.
0.75 ct. faceted red Beryl
1.3 x .9 x .6 in. red Beryl specimen
Utah

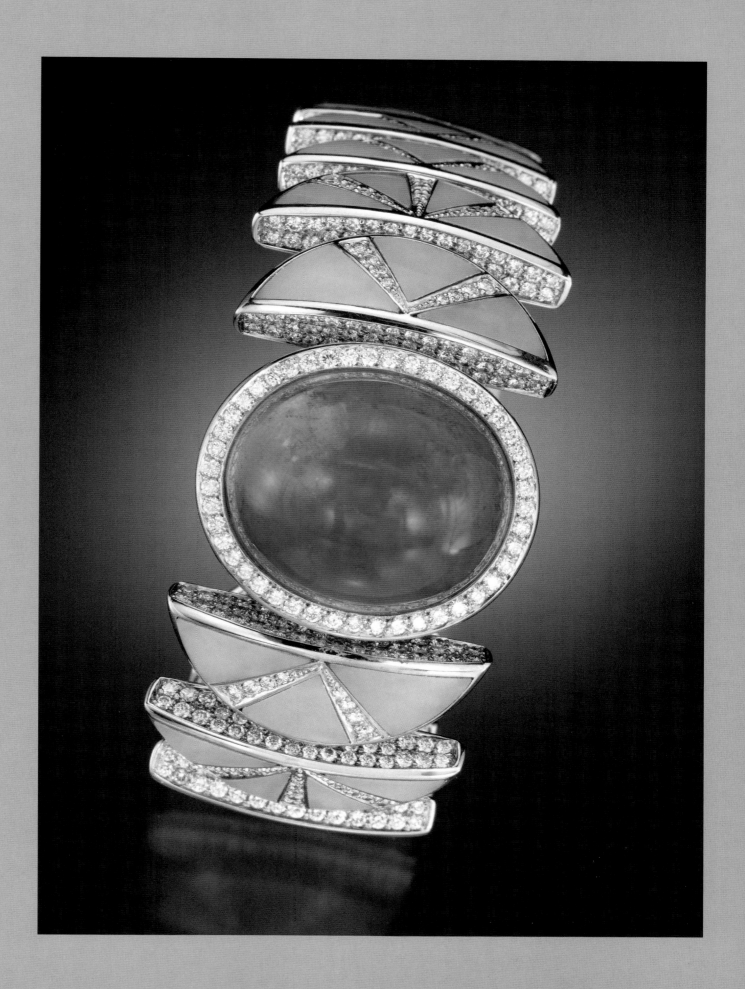

"Treasure of Gachala"
This heafty bracelet features 83.29 ct. Emerald cabachon and
is accented with 522 brilliant cut Diamonds with a total
weight of 12.48 ct. The delightful pink inlay is an opal-like
mineral from Mexico named Palygorskite that is sometimes
called by the misnomer "Pink Opal."
Silverhorn, Santa Barbara, California

DEMANTOIDS, TSAVORITES, AND OTHER RARE GARNETS

Garnets are a very complex group of gems that aren't always red; in fact, garnets can be any color except blue. The two most desirable species of garnet, demantoid, and tsavorite are both green. Green demantoids from the Ural Mountains of Russia have been highly sought after in fine jewelry since the mid 19th century and were a favorite of designer Carl Fabergé. Demantoids have the appearance of green diamonds because of their unusually optical properties. In the late 1960's, an emerald green grossularite garnet was discovered in northern Tanzania and was named by Tiffany & Co. "tsavorite" after the nearby Tsavo Game Park in Kenya. There are many other species of garnets, each with its own color range. Grossulars, however, particularly those from East Africa, seem to exhibit the greatest diversity of color. Another very popular and relatively new to the commercial gem world is the orange species known as spessartite. These spessartites are best known from Brazil, Namibia, and San Diego County, California.

Tsavorite Garnets
Two of the world's finest and largest
Tsavorite Garnets
45 ct. "Bright" Green
32 ct. "Vivid" Green
Tanzania

Opposite:
Demantoid... Fit for a Czar
Antique Demantoid Garnet Ring,
circa 1850, surrounded by 10 rose
cut Diamonds
8.67 ct.
Ural Mountains, Russia

All Colors except Blue!
Colors of Garnet
2 to 25 ct.
Russia, Tanzania, Namibia, and the United States

Demantoid Butterfly
Matched set of 330 Demantoid Garnets from Ural Mountains,
Russia with 472 Diamonds in a unique Titanium mounting so
that the whole piece weighs less than one ounce.
40 ct. total weight of Garnets
ESG Jewelers, Basel, Switzerland

Mandarin Orange
Dodecahedral Spessartite Garnet
Crystal with Mica on Euclase
Rio Grande Do Norte, Brazil
5 ct. faceted garnet shown for scale

Opposite:
Ramona Orange
This Spessartite Garnet Necklace is 18 in. long with 63 color-matched
Garnets with a total weight of 165 ct. and Diamonds with a total weight of
11 ct. The centerpiece Garnet is from Ramona, California and weights 39 ct.
D'Lanor Jewelers, Carmel Valley, California

PARAIBA AND OTHER TOURMALINES

Tourmaline occurs in almost every possible color and its name is actually derived from an ancient Singhalese Sanskrit word "turamali" that means many colors. Red tourmaline is known as rubellite while blue is known as indicolite and the green, verdellite, but one of the most rare tourmalines of all is colorless achroite tourmaline. Because tourmaline is made up of a complex combination of up to a dozen different elements, many of which cause the unique variety of colors, it is extremely difficult to find a colorless gem.

Tourmaline is the most complicated group of gemstones known. Not only do tourmalines have the ability to be any color of the rainbow, depending on their chemical makeup, but can also have several colors in the same stone. Bi-colored tourmalines that are red in the center with green skins are aptly call "watermelon" tourmalines.

Recently a discovery of tourmaline was made near Paraiba, Brazil that shocked the gem world. These tourmalines owed their color to copper, an element usually not associated with gemstones. The result is a shocking array of greens, blues, and blue-green hues never before seen in a natural gemstone.

Opposite:
Blue Paraiba Tourmalines
104 ct. 50 x 15 x 15 mm
crystal
Paraiba, Brazil
4 ct. faceted gemstone
shown for scale

"Electric" Paraiba Tourmalines
This locality has produced the finest and rarest Tourmalines in the world.
9 to 26 ct.
Paraiba, Brazil

Colors of Tourmaline
8 to 154 ct.
Worldwide Localities
1 ct. Diamond shown for scale

Multicolored Tourmaline Crystals
Up to 5 in. long
Brazil, the United States, Afghanistan, and Nigeria

TANZANITE

Tanzanite is one of our newest gemstones. It was originally discovered near Merelani, in the shadow of Mt. Kilimanjaro in Tanzania by Maasai herdsmen in 1968, hence its name. Except for minor occurrences in Kenya, tanzanite has never been found anywhere else. The most familiar color for tanzanite is violetish-blue, although it is naturally "trichroic" or blue, red, or brown depending on which of three crystallographic directions the stone is viewed. Almost all tanzanite is heat treated to eliminate the brown and leave the stone with its familiar blue color. Very rarely, tanzanite has been found in other colors, particularly green. These stones are so rare that few people know they exist.

Tanzanite is not as hard as would be expected for a gem used commercially in jewelry. Its hardness is 6.5, and a hardness of at least 7.0 is usually thought of as the threshold for jewelry use. Therefore, tanzanites should be used in only earrings or pendants; or set in a well-protected ring setting.

Opposite:
Natural Beauty
Gem quality Tanzanite Crystal
4 x 2.5 x 2 in. and 1600 ct.
1 and 10 ct. faceted stones
shown for scale

Colors of Tanzanite
11 to 63 ct.
Merelani, Tanzania

"Queen of Kilimanjaro"
Created as the feature piece for this Bowers' Exhibition, this Tiara features the world's largest faceted Tanzanite of 242 ct. and is accented with 803 brilliant cut Tsavorite Garnets with a total weight of 32 ct. and 913 brilliant cut Diamonds with a total weight of 14 ct. on a 18 kt. White Gold rolled ribbon 8 x 7 x 3 in. and overall weight just 9 oz.
Silverhorn, Santa Barbara, California

DIAMONDS

Diamonds are one of our only windows to the earth's inner structure. They are formed about 100 miles below the earth's surface and have come to the surface in very unusual volcanoes known as "kimberlite pipes". Diamonds are one of the hardest materials known to man, and are many times harder than the next hardest mineral, corundum.

It's important to note that while diamonds are the hardest substance known to man, they aren't necessarily very durable. Diamonds are pure carbon and therefore burn at the relatively low temperature of 700° C., and possess distinct cleavage, which allows them to break or "cleave" easily when struck in just the right direction. Because of their hardness, diamonds will not polish on existing crystal faces.

Most diamonds are filled with inclusions and are black or dark brown in color. However, when diamonds are free from imperfections and devoid of any color, they are considered one of the purist and rarest gems on earth. The only diamond rarer than a flawless and colorless one is a "fancy colored" which opens up a whole new world including sapphire blue, such as the Hope Diamond, and rarest of all, the purplish-red diamond. A one-carat red diamond once sold for $1,000,000! Color in diamonds is caused in a variety of ways, including impurities and structural imperfections.

Opposite:
Octahedral Diamond Crystal
A completely terminated and slightly twisted crystal with trigons on natural unpolished crystal faces. Man has not aided nature by polishing these natural surfaces
25 ct.
Sierra Leone

Common Diamond Colors
Black is the most common color of Diamond. Relatively common are light Yellow and light Brown. Colorless, "H" color shown here, is not as scarce as most people would like to believe. White is the least common of the "common" colors of Diamonds.
1 to 5 ct.
Worldwide localities

Opposite:
The RAREST Diamonds
Diamonds do come in "Sapphire" Blue, "Canary"
Yellow, "Cognac" Orange and "Peridot" Green.
Red Diamonds are the rarest of all, but are too
purplish to be mistaken for Rubies.
0.17 to 2.06 ct.
Worldwide localities

One Inch Cubic Diamond Crystal
Surfaced with triangular growth features
known as trigons, the cubic shape is one of
the rarest forms of gem quality Diamond.
156 ct.
Ghana
1 ct. Diamond shown for scale

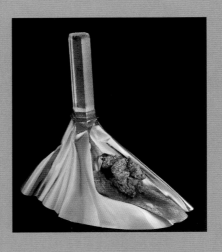

JOHN MARSHALL, SILVERSMITH

IDAR-OBERSTEIN

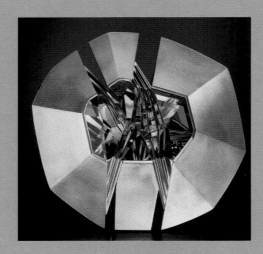

BERND MUNSTEINER, FANTASY CUTS

PART II
GEMS AND
THE SCULPTOR

Gem materials that occur in large sizes such as jade, varieties of quartz, tourmalines, and other pegmatitic gemstones have been carved into various types of sculptures since at least the time of the Romans in Europe and Han Dynasty in China. The Romans extensively used agate to carve cameos, bowls, and cups. The early Chinese used jade and other gem materials mostly for ceremonial objects.

Perhaps the ultimate in gemstone carving was undertaken in the late nineteenth century by Carl Fabergé in Russia with much of his work subcontracted to colleagues in the small village of Idar-Oberstein, Germany. Today, the spirit of Fabergé lives on in this dynamic gem center with such greats as Munsteiner, Dreyer, Zimmerman and others. The Idar artists are best known for their exquisite figures of various animals usually made from varieties of quartz such as agate. Sometimes opal, ruby, chrysoprase, labradorite or other materials are used.

Bernd Munsteiner, however, has set himself apart from his fellow artists, by developing his own unique style of sculpture that is known around the world as simply "a Munsteiner". Silversmith John Marshall of Seattle, Washington is included here because of his incredible use of rough gem crystals as an integral part of his magnificent silver sculptures. These crystals are important on their own but combined his the talented silver work they become unique works of art.

Gem sculptures are very important in any gem collection because they reflect some of man's earliest use of gem materials. The Scott Collection, as with so many aspects of the collection, includes many world-class examples of a quality and diversity not seen anywhere else in the United States.

John Marshall, Silversmith

Seattle Opera House, 1987: Arriving early, I dashed up to the General Director's Room. Coffee was not set up yet in this large almost empty room, with three very becoming display cases in one corner. "Growth Cycle" demanded my total attention. With only one other person in the room, I introduced myself and asked if he knew who the artist was. "It is I, John Marshall" was the reply. A few years later John was commissioned to design and produce our first piece "Dynamic Symmetry". The question arose as to how to mount the sphere. Would the artist accept working on a "simple" stand, which would be secondary to the attention that the star demanded? His professionalism prevailed and the stand totally complemented the sphere in "Dynamic Symmetry". It is still one of my favorite pieces. This unusual artwork demonstrates John's artistic skill as he reveals the exquisite beauty of the gemstone to its best advantage. This merger of silver and gemstones into large sculptures is believed to be a first of a kind.

John Marshall was born in Pittsburgh, Pennsylvania, where he first exhibited an interest in art. After a brief stint in the military, John attended classes at the Carnegie Institute of Technology followed by the Cleveland Institute of Art. Here he further developed his interest in silversmithing and design. John became an instructor at the School of Art, Syracuse University, New York, until he joined the facility of the University of Washington in Seattle. He achieved full professorship there in 1975 and has recently retired. John's work in metal has been widely exhibited at museums and galleries worldwide.

To quote John, "I have always been focused on change, both through concept and process, dictated by my control. Michael Scott brought a fresh light to my work through emotion and spirit. This put me into more of a listening posture to begin my creative experience. The challenge was in bringing the art form to a final stage that performed a marriage between the object and my aesthetic agreement. I still feel as though I am scratching the surface. I am still listening."

Opposite:
"Dynamic Symmetry"
Silver Sculpture, 10 x 10 x 6 in. overall, featuring the world's largest
Rose Quartz Star of 5500 ct., 3.6 in. in diameter from Brazil
John Marshall - 1990
Seattle, Washington
1 ct. Diamond shown for scale

Opposite:
"Organic Cube"
Silver and Acrylic Sculpture, 16 x 10 x 10 in. overall, featuring:a 22,700 ct., 10 in. long Kunzite Spodumene Crystal from Afghanistan.
John Marshall – 1995
Seattle, Washington

"Sense of the Whole"
Silver Sculpture, 9 x 11 x 11 in. overall, featuring 8900 ct., 12 in. long, naturally split and healed doubly terminated Heliodor Beryl Crystal from the Ukraine.
John Marshall - 1993
Seattle, Washington

"Serpent"
Sterling Silver and Mokume-Gane Sculpture,
16 x 16 x 12 in. overall featuring:
16 in. long, 10 lb. Pala Blue Cap Tourmaline
Specimen from California
John Marshall – 1994
Seattle, Washington

Idar-Oberstein

For centuries, the picturesque twin villages of Idar-Oberstein, nestled near the Rhine and Mosel River Valleys in Southwestern Germany, have supported a very important gem carving tradition. Exactly how long this tradition has been maintained in Idar is uncertain, but some believe that it may date back to Roman times. Finely carved cameos made of agate similar to that found in the Idar area, have been found in the Roman ruins at Trier, just a short distance to the west.

Agate and other hard stone carvings has always been Idar's signature. When local mines were nearing depletion, new sources were identified in Brazil and by the late 19th century, very close ties were developed. Idar was now producing hard stone bowls, beads, and even items that were used as popular trade goods by early explorers throughout the African continent. By the early 20th century, Idar was producing sophisticated carvings, particularly animals that graced important places like the Imperial Courts of Russia.

Following World War II, the gem carving and cutting tradition in Idar blossomed. Not only were incredible figurative carvings produced out of even more rare and harder materials such as ruby, but it was also faceting important gemstones, especially from Brazil and Africa. Especially master carver Bernd Munsteiner, who was producing unbelievable gem sculptures like no other, developing new styles of gemstone sculptures. Other sculptures like Dreher, Zimmerman, Petry, and Postler, were developing the more traditional sculptural arts to new heights as well.

The Scott Collection contains some of the finest examples of the Idar carving and faceting tradition known today. Nowhere, in the United States at least, has there ever been a more comprehensive collection with such outstanding quality.

Opposite, Right
"Repose"
Youth in Quartz on Obsidian Base with 18 kt. Gold
Gunter Petry - 1991
Idar-Oberstein, Germany

"Holy Communion"
White Opal from Australia
10.5 x 5 x 1.5 in.
3 1/4 lb. or 7400 ct.
H. Postler – circa 1982
Idar-Oberstein, Germany

Opposite:
Poppy Flower
This delicate Carnelian Chalcedony Quartz
sculpture is the epitome of German lapidary
work.
Gunter Petry – 1992
Idar-Oberstein, Germany

Opposite:
"Mephisto"
Bust from a single Ruby Crystal from Tanzania
with Gold on Obsidian Base
5750 ct.
Dieter Roth - 1991
Idar-Oberstein, Germany

Toad or Frog?
A single piece carved from Ruby & green
Zoisite Rock from Tanzania
2400 ct., 5.2 x 3.3 x 3.2 in.
Gerd Dreher – 1988
Idar-Oberstein, Germany

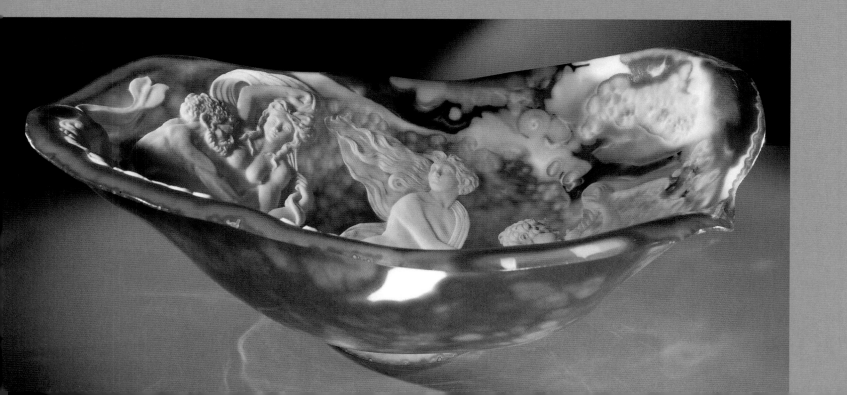

Opposite
"Beautiful Galatea"
A cameo style bowl showing the Agate
form of Chalcedony Quartz
10 x 9 x 3.5 in., 2 lb.
H. Postler – circa 1975
Idar-Oberstein, Germany

Chameleon
Intense green Chrysoprase Chalcedony
Quartz from Kazakhstan on Smokey
Quartz Base
Gerd Dreher – 1992
Idar-Oberstein, Germany

BERND MUNSTEINER, FANTASY CUTS

Bernd Munsteiner is considered one of the foremost gemstone sculptors of our time. He has challenged the traditional norm of lapidary art for over 35 years to place himself apart from other cutters leading to international acclaim and demand for his one-of-a-kind creations.

A third generation gemstone cutter, he began his career as an apprentice at age 14 following conventional cutting and carving methods until he began experimenting with his own unique style. In 1961, he attended the Pforzheim Academy of Design to hone his skills and seek out new ideas for his works. He has built a beautiful studio in the town of Stippshausen near the famed German gem center of Idar-Oberstein.

The "Fantasy Cut" was named for his unique invention that involved making V-shaped groves into the back of the stones. This is technically challenging since most cutting and polishing is done by placing the material against a flat disc. It was a major creative accomplishment.

Mr. Munsteiner has stated that his philosophy for cutting or sculpting a gemstone is to show how human life is reflected in the structure of minerals. He feels that the history of gemstone cutting also reflects our social development and he believes that the future of this art form will depend on innovative and technical designs that not only reflect but also create cultural identity.

Opposite:
"Meditation"
Citrine Quartz and a Gold cone
on a Silver and Smokey Quartz
base
5730 ct.
Bernd Munsteiner – 1987
Idar-Oberstein, Germany

Opposite:
"Natural Movement III"
Smokey Quartz with Rutile on an Obsidian base
10,700 ct.
Bernd Munsteiner – 1987
Idar-Oberstein, Germany

"Impressions"
Smokey Quartz on Frosted Quartz Base
3,400 ct.
Bernd Munsteiner - 1988
Idar-Oberstein, Germany

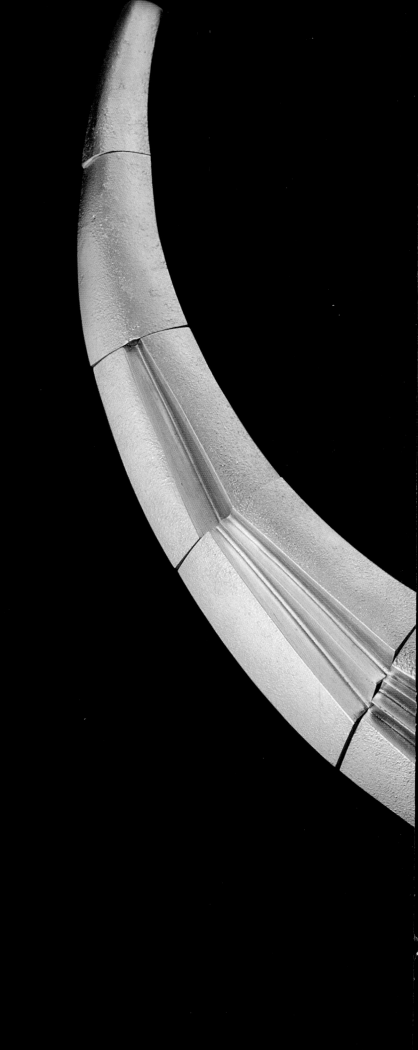

Opposite:
Ametrine
A Collar Necklace featuring a "Fantasy Cut" faceted Ametrine from
Bolivia in White and Yellow Gold. Ametrine is the Amethyst (Purple)
and Citrine (Yellow) varieties of Quartz occurring in the same crystal.
78 ct.
Bernd Munsteiner – 1990
Idar-Oberstein, Germany

"Rhythmus II"
Amethyst Quartz from
Brazil on Marble Base
1160 ct.
Bernd Munsteiner – 1989
Idar-Oberstein, Germany

Opposite:
"Metamorphos"
This human torso size, 214.3 pound or 485,461 ct., meditation piece is believed to be the world's
largest faceted gemstone. Metamorphosed from a one ton Quartz boulder from Bahia, Brazil, its
look shifts continuosly with the viewers changing position.   The golden needles inside are Rutile
crystals, a Titanium mineral, that formed in place just before the clear and colorless Quartz crystal-
lized around them.
Bernd Munsteiner - 1991
Stippshausen, Germany

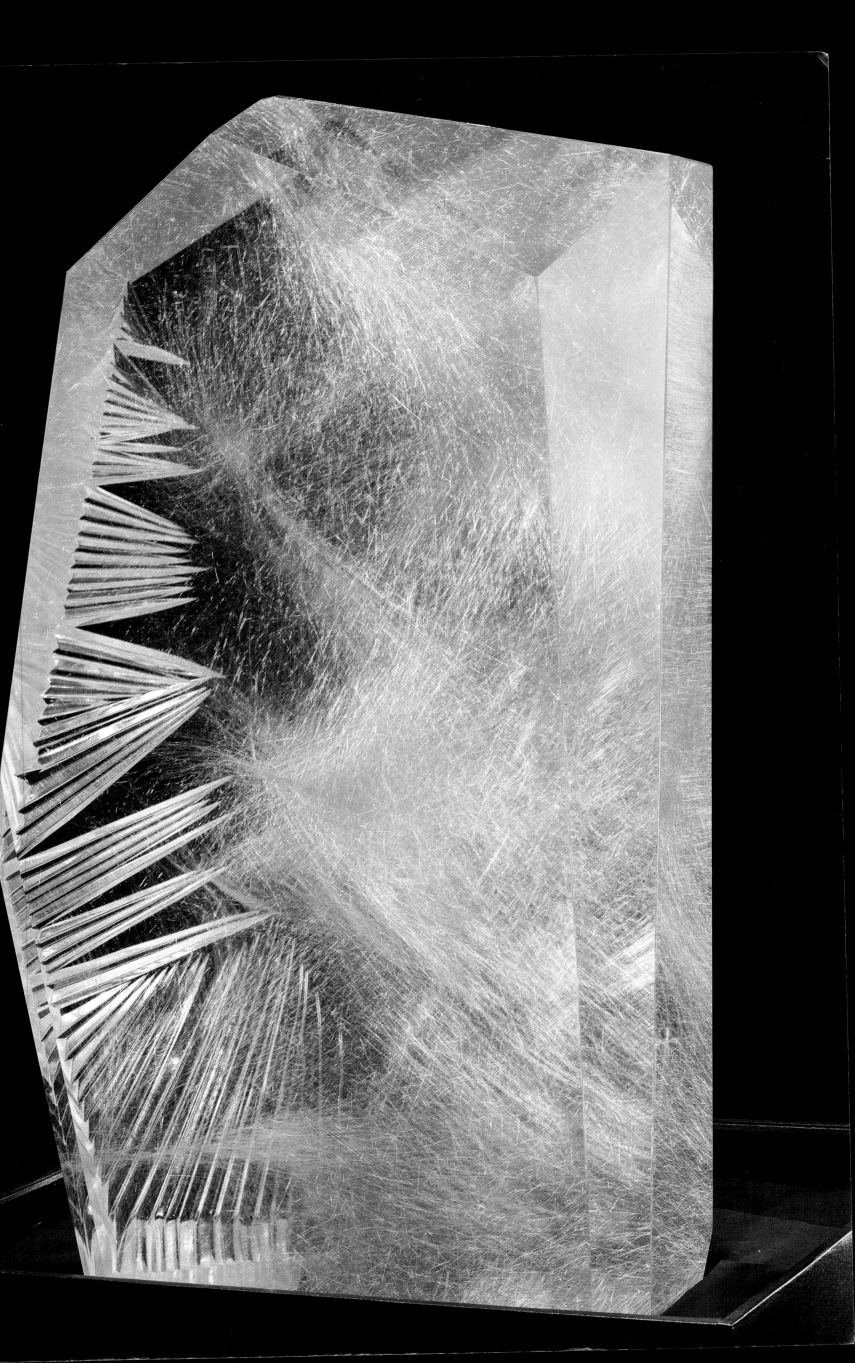